YOUR GUIDE TO INJURY & ACCIDENT CASES IN GEORGIA

LEARN INSIDE SECRETS TO DEAL CONFIDENTLY WITH THE INSURANCE COMPANY, SAVE MONEY AND PROTECT YOUR RIGHTS

JAROME E. GAUTREAUX

WORD ASSOCIATION PUBLISHERS
www.wordassociation.com
1.800.827.7903

Printed in the United States of America.

ISBN: 978 1 63385-150-4

Designed and published by

Word Association Publishers
205 Fifth Avenue
Tarentum, Pennsylvania 15084

www.wordassociation.com

1.800.827.7903

WHY I WROTE THIS BOOK

WHEN PEOPLE ARE INJURED OR LOSE SOMEONE THEY LOVE because of someone else's carelessness, they need answers to some pretty important questions, such as what should I do after an injury? What's my case worth? How does insurance work? How long does it take? How do I find a good lawyer, and not one who's just focused on a quick settlement?

I have heard all these questions from people who have suffered a personal injury or the wrongful death of a loved one. Because I hear the same questions so often, I thought it would be helpful to write this book and try to provide some answers. Sometimes attorneys resist giving away information like this. I suppose they may think that people should hire an attorney to learn the things in this book; however, I think that having good information like this will help you make an informed decision about what to do and how to choose a lawyer who can really help you.

The other reason is a little more personal. I truly care about my clients, and trying to help them through tough times gives me great satisfaction. Yes, I make my living doing it, but it's a lot more than a job to me. If I can change lives for the better, I feel better and I go home feeling like I've done some good in the world. The work is hard, and sometimes tedious, but, ultimately, very satisfying to me. I have had some wonderful clients, and being able to help them gives me great joy.

DISCLAIMER

THE INFORMATION PROVIDED IN THIS BOOK IS DESIGNED TO provide helpful information on the subject matter of personal injury and wrongful death cases. It is not intended to be a substitute for legal advice about your specific case. I urge you to consult with an experienced attorney about your particular case, because every case has its own specific issues and obstacles.

CONTACT ME

I WOULD BE HAPPY TO SPEAK WITH YOU ABOUT YOUR CASE OR a case that your family or friends might have. I also welcome any comments you might have about how this book can be improved. Visit our website to learn more about us and to get more information about injury and wrongful death cases. I wish you the best.

JAROME E. GAUTREAUX

GAUTREAUX & SIZEMORE, LLC

778 Mulberry Street
Macon, GA 31201

Ph: 478-238-9758
Email: jarome@gstriallawyers.com
Website: www.gstriallawyers.com

CHAPTER ONE

INTRODUCTION

JOE AND SUSAN[1] WERE UPSET AND UNSURE WHAT TO DO. A FEW weeks earlier, they had been in a car wreck caused by another driver. They were sitting at an intersection when the other driver blew through a stop sign while talking on a cell phone and struck the driver's side of their car in a "t-bone" type of impact.

Joe injured his neck due to the snapping motion caused by the impact. His doctor told him he may need surgery, but Joe is only 45 years old and is reluctant to have spinal surgery. His medical bills are already in excess of $15,000, he has missed a lot of work (he is an electrician and owns his own business), and their savings are shrinking.

Unlike Joe, Susan was not badly hurt. She was treated and released by a doctor in the emergency room, who prescribed a muscle relaxant and pain medication for her back and shoulders.

"I'M NOT THE TYPE OF PERSON TO SUE."

Joe and Susan did not seek immediate help from an attorney after their accident. As Joe stated, "I'm not the type to sue." He

1 My clients' names have been changed throughout to protect their privacy, but the examples are illustrative of what happens in real cases.

was reluctant to hire an attorney, but he believed he needed help dealing with the other driver's insurance company.

After the accident, the other driver's insurance company kept stalling. They finally offered to pay a small amount of money, but it was barely enough to cover Joe's medical bills and lost wages. At this point, Joe believed he had no choice but to seek the guidance of an attorney in settling the matter.

THE UNFAMILIAR LEGAL WORLD

Even when injured in an accident, as Joe and Susan were, most people would prefer not to seek legal advice. Nearly every client who comes to see me says something like, "I didn't want to have to see a lawyer, but the insurance company was not treating me fairly," or, "I didn't know what to do after my wreck."

There are several reasons why someone might be reluctant to talk to a lawyer about their injury case: It will cost too much money; people don't trust lawyers; the legal system seems unfamiliar; and the language lawyers use can seem almost intentionally unclear to a person who is not trained in the law.

Later on, I will help you to understand the fee structure for personal injury cases, often referred to as contingent fees. I will also provide guidance on how to choose a trustworthy and competent lawyer. For now, let's talk about the legal world and why it can feel intimidating to some.

Understanding the legal world is similar to understanding any other unfamiliar situation that one may encounter. It's how I felt when I was asked to coach my sons in soccer. I grew up playing basketball, baseball, and football, and as in many cities in the south, our hometown didn't even have a soccer league when I was a teenager. I knew as much about soccer as I did about polo, which was close to nothing at all.

I had no idea about how to coach soccer and was apprehensive about doing so. I talked to friends who played soccer, I read the rules of soccer, and I watched videos of soccer games on YouTube. After a while, I became more comfortable with the game and was able to coach matches without totally embarrassing myself. At least the other parents were kind enough not to be too critical. I really enjoy soccer now and can watch a match without wondering what an "off-side" is.

Those injured in an accident also enter an unfamiliar world, that in which the language—legal terms like *res ipsa loquitor* or *respondeat superior*—is unfamiliar and off-putting. Have you ever become irritated when a doctor uses words like *chronic* instead of *long-term* or *anterior* instead of *front*? Unfortunately, the same thing happens when a person is injured and thrust into the legal system for resolving disputes. It can be like trying to understand an entirely different culture and language.

THE DECK IS STACKED AGAINST YOU

Injured people and their families face other difficulties as well. The sources of confusion and irritation go way beyond unclear terminology. Injured people are usually dealing with insurance companies who have teams of adjusters, claims handlers, investigators, and lawyers working for them. The insurance companies have unlimited data and case analysis to help them decide how much to pay for an injury claim, if they choose to pay anything at all. Unlike the insurance companies, most people have no idea how the process works after an injury or death of a loved one caused by carelessness or negligence. The deck can seem stacked against them.

As a lawyer who handles injury and death cases, I know that the need for good information about the whole process is great. My goal is to provide clear, practical information to help people feel more comfortable and confident, and to help them level the playing field with the insurance companies. There is no good reason to allow an insurance company or large corporation to take advantage of someone who has been injured through no fault of their own.

There is another practical reason for this book, however, and that is to save you money. If you have a basic understanding of insurance, the claims process, and injury lawsuits, it can help save you thousands of dollars. Consider this: Two people are involved in similar accidents and suffer similar injuries. One of the individuals purchased Uninsured Motorist (UM) coverage, but the other did not. The one who purchased UM coverage can come out tens of thousands of dollars ahead of the person who did not. We'll talk more about insurance coverage in later chapters.

HOW THIS BOOK CAN HELP YOU WITH YOUR INJURY

This book isn't about legal theory or vague generalities; instead, it is very practical. It will cover common questions about personal injury, insurance, the claims process, and lawsuits involving personal injury or wrongful death. It is meant to be a nuts-and-bolts type of guide to help ease the anxiety and stress often associated with personal injury and wrongful death.

The chapters are arranged chronologically, starting with things you and your family can do now to protect yourselves from financial hardship if you are injured. Planning now can save you thousands later. Like anything else in life, careful preparation can ease future stress and financial strain.

Later chapters will cover what to do after the injury or accident, how insurance is involved, how the claims process works, and how the lawsuit process works in injury and death cases.

No book can cover every nuance of every case, so please keep in mind that every case is different, and only you and your attorney can decide how to proceed in each individual case based on that case's particular facts. The information provided herein addresses common problems and recurring issues; however, please don't think of it as a substitute for a personal consultation with an attorney about your specific case.

CHAPTER SUMMARY:

1. Injury claims and cases can be complicated and a bit intimidating.

2. A basic understanding of the whole process can ease your stress, level the playing field, and save you a lot of money.

CHAPTER 2

WHAT IS A PERSONAL INJURY CASE? FACTS AND FANTASY

Moms and dads, sisters and brothers, sons and daughters—all of them have worried with me, endured tough trials with me, fought insurance companies with me, and shed tears with me about the preventable death of a loved one or the terrible injuries that could (and should) have been avoided.

Personal injury cases are just that: when a person is injured in some way, or when a person loses his or her life due to someone else's careless conduct. These cases are different from property damage cases, such as when your car is damaged in a wreck, or contract disputes, such as when a business or person claims that someone broke a promise to do something. When a contractor, for example, doesn't do the job he promised to do, it may give rise to a contract dispute. If a driver runs a stop sign, though, and hits your car and you break your arm, then you have a personal injury. If the injury is so severe as to cause death, then it is a Wrongful Death case. Sometimes injuries caused by wrongful conduct are called torts, from the Latin term *tortus*, but we can just think of a tort as an injury or death caused by wrongful or careless conduct.

TYPES OF PERSONAL INJURIES

Personal injury and wrongful death cases come in many different forms and include many types of conduct: a wonderful young man dies in an ATV rollover; a loving and devoted father of four suffers horrible burns when a defective industrial product explodes. Consider the truck driver who crashes into a car carrying a family on their way to drop the kids off at school; the young man who falls to his death when a lift falls over; the grandmother who loses both legs below the knees after being neglected in the emergency room. As a lawyer who handles injury and wrongful death cases, I have seen all these situations and many more. The toll these cases take on the families and their loved ones is enormous, and their pain never really ends.

As noted, personal injury cases are quite varied. Some cases involve less severe injuries, but even cases involving minor injuries can cause great inconvenience and suffering. From car wrecks, to trip and falls, to workplace accidents, injuries can happen anywhere and at any time. If an injured person is the sole or primary source of income for his or her family, the doctor visits and lost time from work can cause an immediate financial hardship for the family.

These are all examples of personal injury and wrongful death cases. Some people look at these cases as an easy way for the injured party to make a lot of money, but that view and the reality of personal injury cases are oceans apart.

REALITY VERSUS FANTASY

Personal injury cases are not always easy to pursue; that is, it isn't easy to get fair and full compensation for an injured person. This is because insurance companies can, and often do, make the process difficult. After all, the injured party is often seeking money from an insurance company, and the insurance companies usually prefer to keep that money.

Remarkably, the public seems to have just the opposite view of injury and death cases. They tend to believe that when someone is injured in a car wreck, for example, that either the insurance company quickly surrenders and eagerly writes a check, or the injured party sues and the jury awards them an unjustified wheelbarrow full of cash.

Why do you think reality and public perception differ so greatly? To believe that juries are out of control or that insurance companies just roll over and pay out large sums of money whenever someone is hurt requires many other false beliefs. You would have to believe that insurance companies are foolish and don't care about their shareholders' or policy holders' money. You would have to believe that lawyers for insurance companies are incompetent in court and that juries are easily fooled and can't wait to award a mountain of cash to the injured party. And don't forget the judges, who would have to be standing by and letting these frivolous cases result in huge verdicts. Of course, despite what we hear from the media and the insurance companies, none of this is true. None of this really makes sense.

But the myth persists. The fantasy and the reality are so different that I wonder how so many people could be so wrong. The reality is that our judges generally control cases and apply the rules of evidence and procedure fairly so that everyone gets their day in court; juries are hardly enthusiastic about handing down unjustified verdicts; and insurance companies spend a lot of time and money analyzing cases and hiring talented lawyers to defend cases in court so they don't overpay.

These are not just my views based on the personal injury cases I have handled. Following are a few statistics from the Center for Justice and Democracy (www.centerjd.org) that prove our civil justice system works well and that juries are not making bad decisions: Only about 10 percent of those who are injured file a claim for compensation, and only about 2 percent file a lawsuit. Civil tort case filings have declined, and only about 3-7.5 percent of all civil caseloads were tort trials.[2]

Overall, this gives you a general idea of how personal injury cases work and the reality of the system in place to handle such cases.

Chapter 3 addresses what you can do now to protect yourself and your family before you are injured.

CHAPTER SUMMARY:

1. Personal injury cases include many different types of injuries, such as injuries from car and truck wrecks, medical negligence, workplace injuries, slips, trips, and falls, and defective or dangerous products.

2. Despite the mountain of misinformation that makes it seem as if personal injury cases are easy, the opposite is true. Neither insurance companies nor judges nor juries give away unwarranted compensation to injured people, so we have to be prepared to pursue these cases diligently to obtain fair compensation.

---

2 https://centerjd.org/content/fact-sheet-civil-tort-and-medical-malpractice-caseloads

CHAPTER 3

THINGS TO DO BEFORE YOU OR A LOVED ONE ARE INJURED

CAN YOU BELIEVE THAT THE VERY SAME INJURY CAN HAPPEN to two different people, but one person can come out thousands or tens of thousands of dollars ahead because she was better prepared? I want to help you prepare now so that you can avoid the loss of thousands of dollars if you or a loved one is injured. In wrongful death or permanent injury cases, millions of dollars may be at stake.

Most importantly, be mindful and careful when carrying out your daily habits and routines. This advice may sound obvious, but injuries sometimes occur when people are in a rush or simply do not take practical steps to be safe. Whether at work, at home, on the road, or in the hospital, remember to take just a few common sense steps to minimize your exposure to risk and injury.

For example, handwashing and hygiene can help to stave off many hospital infections, so you should insist that that all hospital personnel wash their hands before examining or touching you or a family member. Following a simple checklist of procedures can greatly reduce infections. Handwashing is one such procedure that all doctors and nurses should do without your having to ask.[3]

We also know that cars can be dangerous when not handled properly, but less noted are the dangers associated with cars that don't involve roadway accidents, such as back-overs, heat-related deaths, and other injuries or deaths related to cars. A wonderful resource covering these types of dangers in depth is kidsandcars.org. Please visit this site to learn the simple steps you can take to protect children in and around vehicles.

In addition to taking some simple everyday steps to stay safe, you may want to consider buying certain types of insurance that can benefit you financially if you are injured in Georgia or in other states as well. Having the right kinds and amounts of insurance in place can make a huge difference in the outcome for you and your family.

UM Coverage: One type of insurance that you may want to consider is Uninsured Motorist, or Underinsured Motorist coverage, sometimes called UM coverage. This type of coverage kicks in when the person at fault has no liability insurance or has an insufficient amount of liability insurance.[4]

For example, suppose that Alexa is injured in a car wreck. The person who hit her was at fault and had $25,000 in liability insurance coverage. Let's further assume that Alexa did not have UM coverage, and that she had injuries that totaled about $100,000. Alexa is *short* $75,000 in insurance coverage because only the $25,000 liability insurance coverage is available for her injuries.

---

3 http://opinionator.blogs.nytimes.com/2011/04/28/speaking-up-for-patient-safety-and-survival/?_r=0

4 Of course, we also strongly encourage all clients to obtain plenty of liability insurance coverage to protect them in case they are involved in an accident.

Frank was in an almost identical type of wreck, with very similar injuries and medical bills. Unlike Alexa, however, Frank had purchased $75,000 of added-on (also called excess) UM coverage as part of his own car insurance coverages.[5] Frank has a total of $100,000 coverage available for his injuries (the $25,000 liability coverage plus his $75,000 UM coverage).

In these examples, Frank will come out better than Alexa by $75,000 because of the UM coverage he purchased. The point is simple; please think about purchasing UM coverage. We typically advise clients to buy at least $100,000 of "added-on" UM coverage, but more is even better.

Med Pay: Another type of coverage to consider buying is Medical Payments coverage (also called Med Pay). Like UM coverage, Med Pay can usually be included in your auto insurance policy. It is similar to health insurance because it can pay for your medical treatment caused by an auto or truck wreck. It could also save you the burden of co-pays and deductibles that accompany your regular health insurance.

There is still another reason to consider buying Med Pay coverage. Often, when a health insurance company pays for your medical treatment after a wreck, that insurance company wants its money back, sometimes referred to as subrogation or reimbursement. It is difficult, at least in Georgia, for the Med Pay insurer to recover these payments in many liability insurance settlements because of the Complete Compensation rule. That is, in many situations, an injured person will not be legally obligated to repay the Med Pay benefits out of a

5 In Georgia, two types of UM coverage are now available: offset coverage and added-on (also called excess) UM coverage. Without going into detail about the nuances of these different coverages, just think of added-on coverage as UM coverage that adds to the liability coverage. In the example mentioned earlier, the added-on UM results in $100,000 of total available coverage. If the coverage had been the offset type of coverage, the liability coverage would offset the UM coverage and would not be added to it, resulting in a total of $75,000 coverage. As you can see, the added-on coverage is typically the better choice.

settlement because, under the law, the person may not have been "completely compensated" for her injuries by the settlement. As you can see, Med Pay can save you a lot of money on the front end *and* the back end of any settlement; however, this can get complicated, and it is best to consult with an attorney who is experienced in handling these issues.

Other less common coverages can come into play in personal injury cases, but UM and Med Pay are the ones we see most often. Contact your insurance company about adding this coverage to your policy now. We strongly urge our clients in Georgia to do so.

CHAPTER SUMMARY:

1. Stay safe, and use common sense at home, on the roadway, in the hospital, and at work.

2. Consider buying UM and Med Pay insurance coverage.

CHAPTER 4

OVERVIEW OF LIABILITY AND INSURANCE

If we didn't have any legal liability for things like car wrecks, there would be little reason for insurance; that is, if you could not be sued in court when you caused a wreck, then you would not need insurance, other than maybe to cover the property damage to your own wrecked vehicle. So, the place to start with an understanding of the injury claim and lawsuit process is to understand the legal rules that apply to injury cases.

CRIMINAL VERSUS CIVIL LAWS

Generally, our legal rules are divided into two broad areas: civil and criminal. Criminal laws are designed to deter and punish those who commit crimes, like DUIs, shoplifting, and more serious crimes like rape or attempted murder. If you violate a criminal law, you risk going to jail, possibly for a very long time.

Civil laws, on the other hand, are not designed to send people to jail. Usually, people do not go to jail for causing a car wreck, unless serious circumstances are present, such as alcohol or drugs, which also violate criminal laws. Instead, civil laws, which allow someone to sue after they've been injured, are designed to compensate the person who has been injured. For example, there are laws in Georgia that permit a person to sue another person who carelessly caused an injury, whether that injury occurred on the roads, at the grocery store, at work, at the hospital, or elsewhere. With this type of lawsuit, the careless person may be required to pay money to the injured person.

INSURANCE PROTECTION AGAINST LAWSUITS

Individuals and businesses want to protect themselves from the possibility of losing a lawsuit and having to pay out-of-pocket expenses to the claimant. This is where insurance enters the picture. The easiest way to protect yourself is to purchase insurance. In return for a person or company paying premiums, the insurance company agrees to pay for things such as a legal judgment against the insured and legal expenses as well. And, of course, people who are injured by the negligence of others are entitled to fair compensation. Insurance thus serves two goals: protection of the insured person and compensation to the person who was injured.

Let's talk about two very important issues when an injury occurs. First, under the law, is it legal for a person or entity to be sued for the injury? Second, if there is legal liability, is there also insurance coverage that applies to provide funds to pay for the injuries? These are two very different things. You can have liability without insurance and insurance without liability. Keep in mind that just because someone has $100,000 of liability insurance, for example, it certainly doesn't mean that the insurance company will pay that amount.

Let's consider an example. Mark is in his SUV, eating a bagel, and in a hurry to get to work at the computer store where he's employed as a technician. As he looks down to grab his bagel, he veers over the center line and hits a car coming in the opposite direction driven by Pam. Thankfully, the speeds were low and the injuries were not severe.

Here, there is no real question about legal liability. Mark simply was careless and caused the wreck and the injuries to Pam. Because Mark was at fault, Pam has the ability to file a lawsuit against him if she chooses to do so. The law provides Pam with a way to hold the other driver responsible for his negligence.

The law says Mark is responsible, but unless Mark has enough money to pay for all of Pam's injuries, that legal responsibility doesn't mean very much. Pam wants and needs money to pay for her injuries, not just a piece of paper saying Mark is responsible.

This is why insurance is so important. The ability to sue someone doesn't help much if there is no insurance available. Have you ever heard the expression *dry hole*? Some lawyers call this a situation where you have the legal ability to sue someone for an injury, but there is no insurance available, meaning the person does not have enough money in the bank or elsewhere to pay any legal judgment. Without insurance, the court might leave you with a piece of paper that says "You are owed $1,000,000 from X," but that paper doesn't help you much, especially if the person files bankruptcy.

In this example, let's hope that Mark has plenty of liability insurance to cover the accident. If he doesn't, then he may face the prospect of being sued, going to court, having a trial, losing, and then having to pay a large sum to Pam, or he may have to file bankruptcy if he doesn't have enough money to pay for Pam's injuries. Clearly, the best situation is for Mark to have plenty of insurance to protect himself and to compensate

Pam. Hopefully, Pam has purchased both UM and Med Pay coverages on her own policy, just in case Mark failed to buy liability insurance or has too little liability coverage.

Now what happens? Does Pam file a lawsuit? Does Pam sue the insurance company? Is a claim filed first? How does the process work?

These questions will be answered in the following chapters, as we dive a little deeper into the whole process.

CHAPTER SUMMARY:

1. Careless or negligent behavior that causes another person to be injured in a car wreck or in some other way can result in legal liability.

2. Just because someone harms you negligently does not mean there is money available for your injuries. This is why insurance is extremely important—to provide payment for any injuries our actions cause others, and to protect us from the financial consequences of losing an injury case in court.

CHAPTER 5

THE INSURANCE CLAIMS PROCESS

When injured because of someone else's negligence, one of your first reactions might be to file a lawsuit as soon as possible. In some cases, depending on the circumstances, it might be the smart choice. (Filing a quick lawsuit might help to avoid the expiration of the statute of limitations, to obtain certain types of evidence quickly, or to depose—question under oath—a witness who is about to leave the country.)

In most cases, however, after an auto wreck or other accident, the injured person and the person who caused the wreck notify their insurance companies of the accident and start the insurance claims process. Many times, the case may get resolved during that process, without the need for any lawsuit.

It is important to understand the insurance claims process. This chapter will cover the claims process and offer some tips on how to make that process go smoothly.

PHASE 1: NOTICE

Notice is an important concept in many areas of law. Injury law is no different. After an auto wreck or other accident, it is important to let all responsible parties know that there has been an accident and that you may be filing a claim.

WHO ARE THE RESPONSIBLE PARTIES TO NOTIFY?

It depends on the type of accident or injury. For example, after an auto wreck, we generally consider giving notice to the following persons or entities:

- **The other driver's insurance company.** If you didn't get this information at the accident scene, you can get it from the accident report completed by the law enforcement agency that investigated the wreck.

- **Your insurance company.** This should be done immediately, especially if you have Uninsured or Underinsured Motorist (UM) Coverage. This is because under your contract of insurance, you may be required to provide prompt notice of a wreck, and the failure to provide that notice can result in your insurance company denying the claim. This is enormously important, and potentially financially disastrous, so I cannot stress to you strongly enough the need to make sure you comply with your own insurance policy, and all possibly applicable UM coverage, so you are not deprived of that coverage.

> ***Tip:*** *In Georgia and in other states, you may be able to get a copy of the accident report online at www.buycrash.com, but it may be quicker just to get it from the law enforcement agency directly.*

PHASE 2: INFORMATION GATHERING

After the insurance companies and responsible parties involved receive the proper and timely notices, the next phase in the claims process is usually to make sure that you get all the investigative materials and medical treatment you need.

> ***Important:*** *While it may seem to be a very simple process, it can get a little complicated. Suppose the person who caused the wreck was working at the time, or maybe the person was driving a car owned by another family member. In those situations, the employer or car owner may also be legally liable for the wreck, so you may need to give them notice of the wreck as well. Generally, in most cases, notice of the accident is given to all possible responsible parties. It can get a little complicated when trying to determine the parties involved and properly and promptly notifying them.*

INVESTIGATIVE MATERIALS

An investigation normally includes taking photos at the scene of the wreck, all the vehicles involved, any visible injuries, and interviewing witnesses. Often, for more complicated cases such as cases involving big rigs or tractor trailers, the investigation will include an analysis by an expert and a download of all electronically available information.

To ensure that all potentially important evidence is not lost or destroyed, we normally send a spoliation letter to any person or company who may have possession or control over the evidence. This is a letter that tells them to keep the evidence in the same condition it was in at the time of the wreck, and to maintain any other evidence as well, such as video recordings, cell phone records, log books, fuel tickets, and many other items, depending on the type of case.

MEDICAL TREATMENT AND INFORMATION

One of the most important things you can do after a wreck is to seek appropriate medical treatment. Some folks avoid going to the doctor because they may have a hard time paying for it or they cannot take time off work, but this is usually a mistake. The insurance company might conclude that you must not have been hurt if you did not seek medical attention, even though you have a perfectly legitimate reason for not seeking a medical diagnosis or treatment right away.

A client I will call Steve had this sort of problem. He was involved in a wreck in which a dump truck struck his vehicle from behind. His neck hurt immediately after the wreck, but he didn't want to take time off work to go to the emergency room or his family doctor, so he tried to endure the pain, eating pain medicine like candy in order to make it through each day.

When it came time to try to settle his case, the insurance company offered very little because Steve's medical bills were so low. In other words, Steve was punished because he tried to "tough it out" and endure the pain. This is exactly what can happen when an insurance company sees that the medical bills are low, even though the injured person had to endure weeks or months of pain and truly needed medical treatment.

Keep in mind that you may have a legitimate claim for future medical treatment as well. For example, we have clients who injure discs in their necks or backs in an auto or truck wreck. The treatment for injured discs usually includes conservative management at first and later surgery as a last resort. If you are trying to settle your case before you have surgery but your doctor has recommended surgery in the future, then you want to include the estimate of the costs of the future surgery in your claim as well.

PHASE 3: NEGOTIATION

Once you have gotten to the point in your medical treatment where you have recovered as much as possible from your injuries, and you have a full understanding of your injuries and insurance, you would normally enter the final phase of the claims process: the negotiations phase. This is the point at which you offer to settle your claim for a certain amount of money. Keep in mind that a settlement means that you give up your right to sue the person who injured you, so you want to make sure you obtain fair compensation.

Because this phase of the claims process is so important, and often quite complex, I will explain it in the next chapter.

CHAPTER SUMMARY:

1. The claims process usually involves several distinct phases, including providing notice, doing a thorough investigation, getting appropriate medical treatment, and, finally, negotiation.

2. Negotiation usually takes place once the other phases are complete, so you have full information about your injury and the available insurance.

CHAPTER 6

THE NEGOTIATIONS PROCESS

I DOUBT ANY QUESTION IS ASKED OF INJURY LAWYERS MORE than "What is my injury case worth?" It is certainly a fair question, since most people need to know what to expect in terms of compensation for their injuries. This chapter will describe how the negotiations process generally works.

THE LEGAL RULES

The first step in understanding how the negotiations process works is to understand the legal rules that typically apply to an injury case. You need to understand these rules, at least in a general way, because in deciding what they should pay, the insurance companies will take into account what they may have to pay if the case were to go to trial and what a jury might award to the injured person.

The entire negotiations process must take into account what the law says an injured person is entitled to receive for their injuries. In Georgia, as in many other states, the law provides that a person proved to be injured by the negligence of someone else is entitled to receive economic and noneconomic damages for their injuries.

ONE: ECONOMIC DAMAGES (OR SPECIAL DAMAGES)

Economic damages, sometimes called special damages, are easily quantifiable, meaning you can put a specific dollar value on them. These types of damages include the following:

- Medical Expenses
- Lost Wages
- Funeral Expenses
- Property Damage
- Future Medical Expenses
- Future Lost Wages

Scenario: Suppose Karen's arm was broken in a car wreck caused by another driver's negligence. If she missed 10 days from work, where she made $200 per day, then she would have a total of $2,000 in lost wages. Let's say her medical bills totaled $20,000 for the surgery and related therapy and other medical care. She would have what lawyers often call *special* damages of $22,000.

> ***Tip:*** *It is important to keep records of all of your medical visits, medical bills, and time lost from work. It is also helpful to bring all of this information with you when you visit your attorney.*

TWO: NONECONOMIC DAMAGES (OR GENERAL DAMAGES)

Noneconomic damages, often called general damages, are not easily quantifiable, as you cannot just add up a specific dollar-for-dollar amount for them; however, the money is used as a way to compensate for these injuries, including the following:

- Physical Pain and Suffering
- Mental and Emotional Pain and Suffering
- Loss of Consortium
- Value of Enjoyment of Life

Special damages and general damages are added together to make up the total damages in many, if not most, injury cases.

Scenario: If Karen was asking for $10,000 in general damages and she has $22,000 in special damages, then at this point in the negotiation process, she would have claimed $32,000 in total damages.

COMPLICATIONS CALCULATING DAMAGES

Sounds simple, right? Sometimes it is, but insurance companies very often complicate the issue by disputing the amount you are seeking.

Medical Disputes. Insurance companies may dispute your medical bills. They might say that you went to the doctor too often, or that your medical treatment was really for something other than the injuries you suffered in the wreck. In other words, there can be, and often are, disputes about whether medical treatment after an injury resulted from the wreck.

Scenario: After the wreck, Karen visits her doctor to check a suspicious mole on her back, most likely not related to her broken arm in the car wreck. Just because her medical treatment came after her injury doesn't mean that the treatment is related to the injury caused by the accident; however, if the treatment can be shown to be related to the wreck (maybe she is unable to grip things with her hand), then the amount can fairly easily be determined by a simple mathematical calculation.

Quantifying General Damages. General damages are always harder to specify in strict dollar amounts. This is because they can vary so much from person to person and from situation to situation.

Let's consider pain and suffering. A 20-year-old might suffer very little pain from a car wreck, but that same wreck could cause a 70-year-old with osteoporosis a great deal of long-lasting pain. A scar to someone's face causes more suffering than a scar on the bottom of the foot. Generally, the monetary value of pain and suffering takes into account the mental and physical pain and suffering, the duration of the pain and suffering, and the severity of the pain and suffering, but no fixed formula can be provided. Juries use their common sense to arrive at a fair amount for pain and suffering.

COMPROMISE

Everything I've written so far sounds simple in theory, but in application it can be very tricky.

Sometimes insurance companies pay more than they think a jury would award at trial. Sometimes the injured person may accept less than they think a jury would award at trial. So, why would an insurance company pay more and an injured person accept less than the amount they think a jury would reasonably provide in a trial?

Very often it boils down to a dispute of damages, a compromise between the two parties, and neither side knowing for sure what a jury will do. In many personal injury cases, the amount for pain and suffering that should be paid is the subject of dispute; the insurance company and their attorney will try to minimize it, and the injured person and her attorney try to maximize it.

Neither party can be completely sure what a jury will do. For instance, one jury might think an award of $10,000 for pain and suffering is adequate and fair in a case, but if another jury heard the very same case, it might award $25,000 for pain and suffering. The two parties will consider all of this in negotiations, and the final amount will often wind up somewhere in the middle, or close to it, of what both parties actually want. They compromise, and the case is settled for less than the injured person might think they would have been able to get, but is more than the insurance company would have preferred to pay. Neither party knew how much the jury would have awarded, but based on the known damages, and the unknown outcome of a jury trial, both parties accepted more or less than they thought they might have been awarded at trial.

Some clients have told me that the whole process is a bit like buying a car. One side wants to pay less and the other side wants to get more, and through the negotiations process, the parties usually settle on an amount somewhere between the two starting points. This is not a bad way to think about the negotiations process in personal injury cases.

NEGOTIATIONS VERSUS LAWSUIT

Questions that often come up include the following: When do the negotiations take place? Do you have to file a lawsuit before you negotiate? How do you start the process of negotiating?

Every case is different, but some general practices apply to most cases.

In many car wreck and other injury cases, negotiations may occur prior to the filing of a lawsuit. This saves the time and expenses associated with a lawsuit.

In other cases, especially in more serious injury cases, it may take the filing of a lawsuit to convince the insurance company to negotiate. In the years since the market crash of 2008, it seems that in order for insurance companies to offer reasonable settlements, more cases are being litigated. Sometimes we have to pursue cases all the way to trial in order to get an insurance company to pay. In fact, if an insurance company suspects that a certain lawyer doesn't have the time or talent to take a case to trial and handle it properly, how much do you think that insurance company will offer that lawyer? If the insurance company isn't at least a little concerned that it is up against a lawyer who is not afraid to try a case, they may offer less to that lawyer's clients. Big talk is one thing; actual jury trial experience is something else entirely. Ask your lawyer if he or she has tried cases to juries successfully.

MAXIMUM VALUE FOR YOUR CASE

To help our clients achieve maximum value for their injury claims, we like to follow some general guidelines.

First, it is often better to wait until you have completed your medical treatment before you start trying to negotiate with the insurance company.

Tony's case can help you see why you may want to wait until you have completed your medical treatment before you negotiate the value of your injury claim. Tony was injured at a large home repair store when a can of paint fell from a high shelf and struck him in the head. He had some pain and discomfort, and was out of work for a couple days, but he couldn't afford to stay out of work, and he hoped the pain would just gradually go away.

Tony contacted the insurance company for the store to see what they would offer for his injury. He was offered $2,000, and told he had to accept it within a week or the offer would be taken off the table. Tony needed the money, so he took the $2,000 and signed what's called a release, in which he promised not to bring any kind of lawsuit in the future relating to his injury at the store.

You can guess what happened after that. Instead of the pain going away, Tony's neck pain got worse, to the point where he was eating pain pills like candy, and he couldn't sleep through the night without waking up in pain.

Finally, Tony sought medical treatment. An MRI revealed that Tony had injured two of the discs in his neck, and his doctor told him that it was likely due to the can of paint falling on his head, since Tony had no pain or other neck problems prior to the accident. To fix the disc problem, Tony would need surgery and therapy, which would cost about $60,000. He would also be out of work for six weeks.

As you can imagine, Tony was extremely upset and anxious about all of this. He wished he hadn't taken the quick "low-ball" offer from the insurance company. Unfortunately, there wasn't much he could do at this point. He signed a full release and, thus, gave up his right to bring a lawsuit or collect any more money for his injury.

The point is that just a little patience would have made all the difference to Tony. He had a case that was worth in excess of $100,000 that he settled for $2,000. You don't want to settle your case prematurely, so we generally tell clients that it is best to wait until you have finished with your medical treatment before you try to settle.

Second, there are various time limits, such as statutes of limitation, statutes of repose, and others, that can alter the decision about when to negotiate. We must consider all circumstances when deciding the best time to negotiate, but, generally, we prefer that our clients finish their medical treatment before trying to settle their cases.

CHAPTER SUMMARY:

1. Negotiations involve trying to determine how much your claim is worth under the law.

2. We usually advise clients to wait until they finish their medical treatment before attempting to settle.

CHAPTER 7

FINDING A LAWYER TO HANDLE YOUR INJURY CASE

I AM NOT THE TYPE OF LAWYER WHO TELLS EVERY INJURED person to run out and hire a lawyer. When the consequences of making a mistake are very small and not financially risky to the injured person, then it is possible for the case to proceed without a lawyer.

Many folks, however, try to handle their injury claim on their own when they should have at least consulted with a lawyer to see if the case was more complicated than they originally thought. Many clients have shared sad stories about trying to handle cases on their own in which they encountered problems. Sometimes, though not always, this can limit our ability to get full compensation for their injuries.

For example, many folks don't know how to decide what the special damages are. They don't know if it's based on the total medical bills, the amount paid by insurance, or some other amount. They don't know whether they should include their total lost wages or just the amount they lost after they used all their vacation and sick leave. You don't want to agree on a settlement amount from the insurance company without knowing fully the compensation to which you are entitled.

They may also not be aware of the increasingly complex and changing rules that determine whether their health insurance company is entitled to reimbursement or repayment of any amounts it paid for their medical treatment caused by an injury.

Imagine that you were hurt in an accident and that your health insurance company covered $30,000 of your medical treatment. Let's also assume that you settled your injury claim for $100,000. You settled the case without worrying about the health insurance company's request for repayment of the $30,000 it paid for your medical treatment. And now your health insurer writes you a nasty letter, telling you that it is cutting off your health benefits and suing you in federal court.

That doesn't sound like much fun, does it? Health insurers definitely seem to be getting more aggressive about getting their money back from settlements; however, the applicable law determines whether they are actually entitled to reimbursement. The problem for most people is that the law is complicated and often unclear in this area. Even lawyers don't always agree on when a health insurance company is entitled to reimbursement from an injured person's settlement. The main point is, this is an area where an experienced lawyer may be very helpful. You don't want to get stuck with a huge bill or lose your health benefits after a settlement.

Usually, consulting with a personal injury lawyer does not cost anything. I meet with clients all the time, free of charge, and tell them if I think they would be better off handling the case on their own or if I think I could get them a better settlement by handling it for them.

I am often asked for referrals to other lawyers who handle cases that we don't handle. Clients ask us to refer them to criminal defense lawyers, probate lawyers, business lawyers, and many others. We look for certain qualities in lawyers that injured people may want to consider, as well when they have to decide which lawyer to hire for their injury case.

The one thing I caution my clients about is lawyers who advertise on TV. Just because a lawyer advertises on television does not mean they are the best lawyer for your case. Any lawyer can pay for television advertising, so this might not be the most reliable way for you to choose representation. I'm not suggesting that you avoid a lawyer who advertises; rather, I would simply urge you to consider other important factors as well.

I would not choose a doctor, a plumber, or an electrician because they advertise on television, but I wouldn't avoid them for that reason either. Instead, I would look at more objective factors, such as other satisfied customers or patients, their years of experience, how well they handle a request, and other similar objective factors. Popularity does not equal competence.

Following are the qualifications I would look for if I were hiring a lawyer for my own injury case:

1. Did you do well in law school? Were you on the law review or moot court board?

2. Have you actually tried any cases to juries? How many? How many did you win?

3. Have you written any published books, articles, or papers, especially any that were part of a legal education program?

4. Do you teach, or have you taught, any actual law school or legal courses?

5. Do other lawyers ask you to help them with their cases?

6. Have you won any legal awards?
7. Will you personally be handling my case, or will it be your assistant or paralegal?
8. What is your policy on phone calls? Will you return my calls promptly?
9. How much do you charge?
10. What have other clients thought about the way you handled their case?

HOW MUCH WILL MY CASE COST?

Let's elaborate on the question of cost. Most personal injury lawyers I know charge their clients based upon a percentage of the amount recovered in the case. This fee can range from one-third of the total amount recovered to fifty percent and above for more complicated cases such as medical malpractice, products liability, or governmental liability cases. This allows a person to hire a lawyer without having to pay the lawyer by the hour, but the fee is a matter of contract and the ethical rules governing lawyers. The fee should be reasonable and fair, and you should make sure that you understand exactly how the fee is determined.

The same thing is true for expenses. Personal injury cases can be very expensive. We have handled medical malpractice and dangerous product cases where the expenses exceeded $100,000 by the time the jury got the case, and yet other cases have had expenses as low as $500. Make sure you understand how the expenses are determined.

Will the lawyer pay your expenses at the outset and expect reimbursement at the time the case is settled? If so, do the expenses come out of the lawyer's portion or your portion of the recovery? These are the types of things you should know when you hire a lawyer to handle your injury case.

You will likely want to know what happens if the case is lost, the attorney withdraws, or you decide to fire the lawyer. These are all important considerations.

Finally, be sure to get a written contract from the attorney. It should state clearly all financial matters, including fee, expenses, and who is responsible for paying what. At our firm, we provide our clients with a written agreement and a letter, so that they know exactly how we handle the financial matters.

CHAPTER SUMMARY:

1. While it may not always be necessary to hire a lawyer for some smaller cases, it may be necessary to hire a seasoned lawyer with trial experience for the more serious and complicated cases.

2. We urge folks to look at the objective factors that really show how qualified a lawyer is before hiring that lawyer, just as we do when hiring other professionals in their fields.

3. We always recommend having a contract with your lawyer that clearly states what you will be responsible for paying when your case settles, and what the lawyer's fees and expenses will be.

CHAPTER 8

THE LAWSUIT

WHAT HAPPENS IF YOUR CASE CANNOT BE SETTLED FOR A reasonable amount? If the insurance company or companies involved do not offer an adequate amount to settle your case, then you may have to file a lawsuit.

The previous chapter discussed choosing a lawyer. While you don't have to hire a lawyer to handle your lawsuit, I have never seen anyone without legal training properly handle a lawsuit and achieve a good result, except in extremely small cases, typically worth less than a couple thousand dollars in small claims court. For almost all injury cases, it makes sense to consider hiring a qualified attorney who has experience in handling all kinds of injury cases.

Filing a lawsuit can cause anxiety for clients, because they envision having a full-blown trial with a judge and jury, but that isn't always the case. There's a lot more to it.

Complaint: A lawsuit starts with the filing of a complaint with the court, and it typically details why the person who is suing (called the plaintiff) thinks the other person (called the defendant) is liable for their injury.

Summons: After the complaint is filed, the person or people being sued (the defendants) are given a copy of the complaint along with a notice from the court that they have been sued. This notice is called a summons, because it is the court's way of letting you know that you have been sued and are now required to follow the rules for responding and dealing with the lawsuit.

Answer: An answer is the response to the complaint, and it is just as the name implies. An answer responds to what the plaintiff asserts in the complaint. Typically, the answer says that most of what the plaintiff asserts is just not correct. Other defenses are also usually asserted in the answer, including things like the expiration of the statute of limitations (the legal amount of time someone has after an injury to file a lawsuit), or the plaintiff is at fault, or someone else is at fault.

Discovery: After this initial exchange, the parties will usually conduct discovery. This is the longest part of most lawsuits. Each side gets a chance to ask written questions, obtain documents, and take depositions, where people answer questions under oath. Scheduling all of this activity takes time and persistence. This is the phase of the case where each side tries to develop the evidence in its favor. Some folks believe the trial is when the lawyers find out the facts, but there are few surprises in most civil trials, because most of the facts have been revealed in discovery by the time the case gets to trial.

Trial: Finally, once discovery is completed, the case may then proceed to an actual trial. In some busy courts, it can take months just to get a case scheduled for trial.

Keep in mind that at any point during this whole process, even after the lawsuit commences with the filing of the complaint, through the time the trial is completed, the case can be settled. In fact, most injury cases that are filed in court are settled before trial begins. So, just because a case is filed in court does not mean that a trial is necessary or imminent.

In addition to these basics, the handling of a lawsuit requires many strategic decisions. When should a certain person be deposed? What are our weak points, and what are the other side's weak points? Which documents are most important? In what order should we present our case? What is the case worth? How much expense will be involved? An experienced lawyer will be able to make these decisions in consultation with his client throughout the process. The case is your case, and you should be sure you know what is going on, keeping in mind that the process is often frustratingly slow and tedious.

CHAPTER SUMMARY:

1. A lawsuit may be required if your case can't be settled fairly.

2. Lawsuits take time and effort, but if done well, can result in a favorable outcome.

CHAPTER 9

TRIALS AND APPEALS

YOU COULD FILL A LIBRARY WITH BOOKS THAT DISCUSS TRIALS. If you have filed a lawsuit and gone through discovery and your case still isn't settled, then a trial is usually the next step.

Most people have an idea of what trials are like from television or movies; however, most real trials are not quite as exciting as the ones you see on screen. Most trials are not very exciting affairs. They contain dry testimony, explanations of complicated documents, and experts explaining technical details to jurors, most of which isn't the stuff of high drama; however, it is very important that clients remain patient and polite throughout the trial, even when they hear things said about them that they know are untrue and mean-spirited. Jury trials are like endurance contests, and great patience and persistence is required.

JURY TRIAL PROCESS

Following is an outline of the way most trials proceed:

> **Jury Selection**: This is the first part of most trials, where the lawyers or the judge (or both) ask questions of jurors to determine if they are a good fit for the case that is being tried.

Opening Statement: Each side summarizes their case in an opening statement. This is an overview of what the case is about and what you are going to prove in the trial.

Witness Testimony: The plaintiff usually puts up all their witnesses first. Lawyers will often use documents and photographs, considered evidence, while questioning the witnesses. The jury sometimes sees the documents, photos, videos, charts, etc., while listening to witness testimony. After the plaintiff has presented their case, the defense gets to put up its witnesses and other evidence. During both the plaintiff and defense cases, each side will have an opportunity to cross-examine each other's witnesses as well.

Judges Instructions and Closing Arguments: After all the witnesses have been examined and the evidence presented, normally the judge will instruct the jury on the law that governs the case, and each side then gives its closing arguments to the jury. It is only after closing arguments that the jury gets to render its decision as to which side wins the case. As was addressed earlier in the book, the jury will typically have to decide several things, including, but not limited to, whether the defendant is liable; that is, whether the defendant is responsible for the injuries; and how much the plaintiff is entitled to receive for medical expenses, lost wages, or income and pain and suffering. In Georgia, the jury's decision in civil cases generally must be unanimous, meaning that everyone on the jury must reach the same decision. Sometimes a jury is unable to decide unanimously which side wins, resulting in what is called a deadlock. This can lead to a new trial in many cases, and the whole process starts all over.

Appeal: After the trial, the losing side may decide it wants to appeal the decision. There are many reasons for an appeal. Maybe the judge told the jury the wrong governing law. Maybe evidence was allowed in that should have been kept out. There are all kinds of reasons a lawyer may advise a client to appeal. One thing is clear; an appeal usually takes a long time, sometimes more than a year after trial, to get a decision from an appeals court.

Clients sometimes believe that once a jury hears their case, they'll surely find in their favor. This is a dangerous belief, like most confident predictions about what may or may not happen. It reminds me of advice some financial advisors give when they say that a stock will certainly increase in value. Overconfidence is rarely justified in trials. Lawyers don't know what juries will do, and I have found that self-described experts rarely can predict an outcome of a jury trial or an appeal.

The most important traits that can help you succeed at trial and appeal are humility, courage, and persistence. Attention to the evidence is also crucial. A lawyer who thinks he or she can just "charm" a jury without good evidence is flat-out wrong and suffering from an inflated sense of his or her own ability. Jurors are smart, and as a group, they are even smarter. They can see through the nonsense and appeals to their emotions. Also, keep in mind that there are no guarantees of any outcome.

Given all this uncertainty, it may make sense to find a lawyer with real trial experience and a background that demonstrates a serious commitment to excellence. Some lawyers seem to think that popularity is the most important attribute for success. Those lawyers certainly are not trial lawyers, because a trial lawyer must cultivate competence, effort, and courage, rather than superficial popularity, to succeed. It takes time and effort to accumulate trial experiences, but those experiences are important in giving lawyers the confidence they need to do a great job representing injured people.

A good lawyer can help you maximize your recovery at any point in the process, from claim to lawsuit to appeal; however, in my opinion, it becomes especially important to choose a lawyer who has real meaningful trial experience to handle a trial for you. Many lawyers can settle a case; fewer lawyers can really try a case well against talented defense lawyers.

CHAPTER SUMMARY:

1. Trials can take a while to complete, and require patience and persistence.

2. A good, experienced lawyer can help you achieve a good result in the trial and appellate process.

CHAPTER 10

BRINGING IT ALL TOGETHER

Our journey together has taken us from the injury, to the insurance claims process, to the lawsuit and appeal. While this process can be confusing and frustrating, a good, basic understanding of claims and lawsuits will help you recover the maximum value for your personal injury case.

The most important thing an injured person can do is to get better. For most people who have to manage work, family, and other commitments, it makes sense to hire an experienced lawyer to deal with the insurance companies, defense lawyers, judges, and experts. While the lawyer is handling these matters, the injured person can fully focus on getting better and recovering from their injuries.

The best way to prepare yourself for an unforeseen accident is to make sure you have plenty of insurance coverage, whether you end up being injured or you cause an injury to someone else.

If you are hurt in an accident, make sure you get proper medical attention, information about the wreck, witness names and statements, and vehicle information, so that you can prove your case.

When you file your claim, be ready for a long process while the insurance companies try to minimize their payments.

When you enter the negotiation phase, be patient and persistent.

If you cannot settle your case fairly, then you may have to file a lawsuit. In this case, it is strongly encouraged that you hire a lawyer to file the lawsuit for you. Again, be prepared for a long process, which will require your cooperation and assistance throughout. Keep in mind that even after a lawsuit is filed, your case still can be settled.

If you win your lawsuit … great! But even then, you may be facing an appeal by the defendant and another long delay.

Personal injury cases can be life-changing events. I hope the information and advice provided herein will help you should you have to deal with a personal injury claim or lawsuit. I wish you the best.

WA